Leo Brouwer

Nuevos Estudios Sencillos

for guitar

Chester Music

Exclusive distributors:

Hal Leonard
7777 West Bluemound Road,
Milwaukee, WI 53213
Email: info@halleonard.com

Hal Leonard Europe Limited
42 Wigmore Street Marylebone,
London, WIU 2 RN
Email: info@halleonardeurope.com

Hal Leonard Australia Pty. Ltd.
4 Lentara Court Cheltenham,
Victoria, 9132 Australia
Email: info@halleonard.com.au

Order No. CH64273
ISBN 0-7119-9304-1
This book © Copyright 2002 by Chester
Music

Music engraved by Michael McCartney

Printed in EU.

www.halleonard.com

Contents

NUEVOS ESTUDIOS SENCILLOS

I

Omaggio a Debussy

Leo Brouwer

Estudio no. 1

Esta colección es para princípiantes o niños (pequeños).

Pequeños arpegios (*p, i, m*) y facilidad de mano izquierda.

Poner atención en la dinámica ($<$ $>$).

Carácter *legato*.

El *tempo* es relativo. ♩. = 100 – 120. No muy rápido.

Study no. 1

This collection is for beginners or children.

This study is for short arpeggios (*p, i, m*) and developing left hand facility.

Pay attention to the dynamic marking ($<$ $>$).

Maintain a *legato* style.

The *tempo* is relative. ♩. = 100 – 120. Not too fast.

II

Omaggio a Mangore

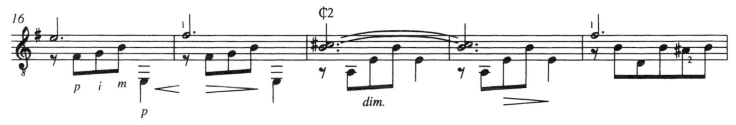

Estudio no. 2

Es un estudio sobre ritmos con pequeñas disonancias.

Observar el contraste de las secciones 1a (algo *staccato*) y 2a (*legato e dolce*).

El trabajo constante es sobre alternancia de p, m (mano der.)
i

Sólo por excepción hay "adelantos" técnicos para el principiante al final con a y rasgueado.
m
i

Study no. 2

This is a study for rhythms and mild dissonances.

Note the contrast between the sections 1a (somewhat *staccato*) and 2a (*legato e dolce*).

The technique of alternating p, m (right hand) is featured throughout.
i

Technical "advances" for the beginner occur only at the end, with the use of a and rasgueado.
m
i

6

III
Omaggio a Caturla

Estudio no. 3

Estudio sobre patrones rítmicos afrocubanos.

Dinámicas de onda ($<$ $>$) y *pulgar* (mano derecha).

Study no. 3

A study on afro-cuban rhythmic patterns.

It also emphasises wave-like dynamics ($<$ $>$) and the right hand thumb.

IV
Omaggio a Prokofiev

Estudio no. 4

Estudio sobre el pulgar.

Mano izquierda en IIe posición.

Contrastes dinámicos (***f*** *marc.* y ***p***)

Importante guardar las articulaciónes de *staccato*, *legato*, y notas más largas y cortas (♩ ♪)

Study no. 4

This is a study for the right hand thumb (*p*).

The left hand is in second position.

Dynamic contrasts (***f*** *marc.* and ***p***)

It is important to observe the articulation marks for *staccato*, *legato*, and the longer and shorter notes (♩ ♪)

V

Omaggio a Tarrega

Comodo

l.v. sempre

mp

(come timpani)

marc.

legato

marc.

marc.

legato

legato

f *marc.* **f** *sempre, intenso e marcato*

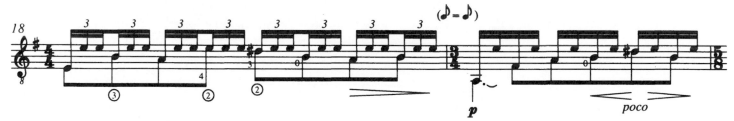

(♪ = ♪)

p

poco

riten.

rit. *ritmico*

Estudio no. 5

Pequeño *tremolo* de 3 notas (prepatorio para 4 notas).

Estilo minimalista con extensiónes temáticas.

Las pausas ritmicas son resonancias, no silentes.

Atención a igualdad de pulsación ritmica (♪ = ♪).

Study no. 5

This study introduces *tremolos* of 3 notes (acting as a preparation for the more usual four note version).

It is in the minimalist style, with thematic extensions.

The notes should be allowed to resonate through the rhythmic pauses, without any silences.

Pay attention to the equality of the rhythmic pulse (♪ = ♪).

VI
Omaggio a Sor

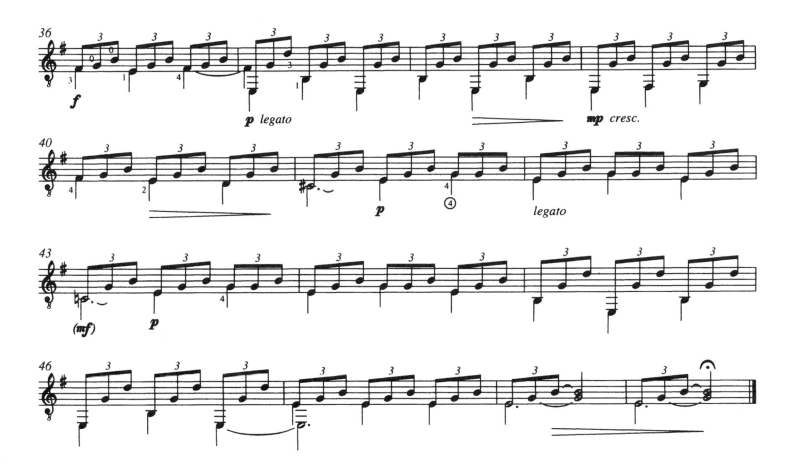

Estudio no. 6

Este estudio de arpegios rectos de 3 notas y el pulgar es sencillo, sólo la sección central - compases 22 al 29 ofrece un cambio al registro agudo (cuerdas primas).

Atender las dinámicas "de onda" ($<$ $>$) para hacerlas gradualmente.

La fórmula del arpegio puede invertirse (*p, m, i*). *Ej. 1*

La fórmula del arpegio puede ampliarse a 4 notas (*p, i, m, a*) con cuerda (1). *Ej. 2*

Study no. 6

This simple study is built up of continuous three note arpeggios with the thumb playing the melody. Only in the central section, at bars 22-29, is the upper register (the top strings) used.

Make sure that the "wave-like" dynamics ($<$ $>$) are executed gradually.

The arpeggio pattern can be inverted (*p, m, i*). *Ex. 1*

The arpeggio pattern can be extended to 4 notes (*p, i, m, a*) by adding the first string. *Ex. 2*

Ej. 1 / Ex. 1   Ej. 2 / Ex. 2

VII
Omaggio a Piazzolla

Estudio no. 7

Para las notas repetidas, acentos y ligados.

El esquema de notas repetidas debe ser tocado de ligero a intenso (mano derecha).

Acentos salen mejor tocando la nota después más *p*, que tocando el acento más fuerte.

Los compases 5 y 6, así como el 13 son contrastantes (*ponticello, staccato*)

La sección D is *p* haciendo *staccato* la última corchea de compas.

Study no. 7

This study is for repeated notes, accents, and slurs.

The repeated note figure should be played moving from a light to an intense touch in the right hand.

Accents come out better by playing the following note more quietly,
rather than by playing the accented note more strongly.

Bars 5 and 6 as well as bar 13 should be contrasted with the others by the use of *ponticello* and *staccato*.

Section D is *p*, with the last quaver of each bar to be played *staccato*.

VIII

Omaggio a Villa-Lobos

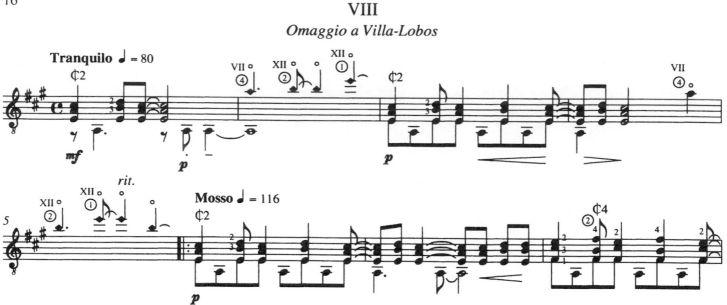

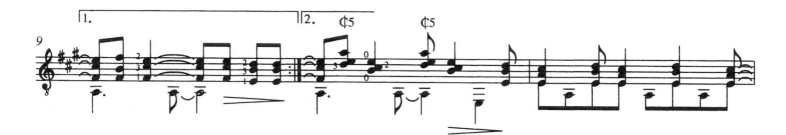

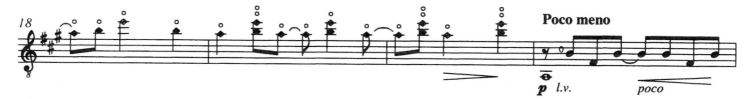

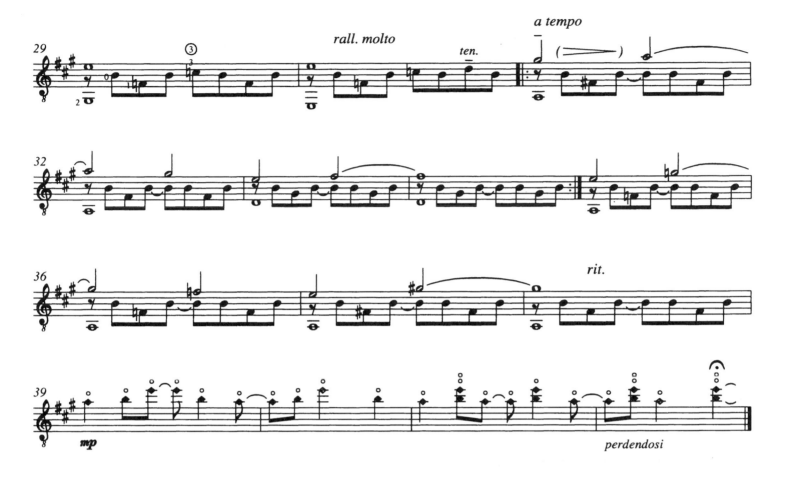

Estudio no. 8

Para acordes, armónicos y pequeña "cejà".

Este estudio puede tocarse en los primeros grados, alcanzando la pequeña cejà.

Los armónicos naturales son muy fáciles y pueden anticiparse en el progreso curricular, añadiendo interés colorístico.

La pequeña cejà sólo ocurre en II, IV y V posición con los cambios de posición preparados.

Study no. 8

A study for chords, harmonics and the partial *barré*.

This can be played by elementary students who are able to manage a partial *barré*.

Natural harmonics are very easy and can be learnt at an earlier stage than usual here, so as to add colour.

The partial *barré* is only employed in II, IV and V positions, and with the position changes prepared.

6a in Fá (opcionalmente)
6th in F (optional)

IX
Omaggio a Szymanowski

Estudio no. 9

Estudio sobre el legato melódico. Para las melodías quebradas.

En B son frases de 2 compases en $<\!\!>$.
poco

Algún salto (compases 5 al 6; 16 al 17; 18 al 19) no impide el *legato* melódico.

Como dificultad no pasa de V posición.

Study no. 9

The object of this study is to maintain a *legato* line in a melody which often moves around in leaps.

At B there are phrases of two bars with wave-like dynamics ($<\!\!>$).
poco

The few changes of position (bars 5-6; 16-17; 18-19) should not be allowed to affect the melodic *legato*.

The technical demands do not require going beyond V position.

X

Omaggio a Stravinsky

Toccata

Estudio no. 10

Este estudio se concentra en las cuerdas graves, ligados y alternancia
de *p* (pulgar) con *i, m (a)*, obligando a la mano derecha a articular en "bloque".

Los 9 compases de A y los 6 de B pueden repetirse cada uno consecutivamente
o el período completo *ad lib*.

Hay recursos compositivos como "caesuras" cortas (') y largas (G.P.) que resultan poco usuales
para principiantes; rogamos al profesor los explique, vale.

La violencia de los acordes permite algún color distinto y *staccato* de izquierda (levantando la cejilla,
lo cual relaja la izquierda tambien. Esta técnica es poco común en la técnica tradicional pero se le
encuentra muchas veces en al jazz.

Study no. 10

This study concentrates on the lower strings, slurs and the alternation of *p* with *i, m (a)*.

The 9 bars of A and the 6 of B can be repeated; either each one consecutively, or the entire period *ad lib*.

There are "caesuras", both short (') and long (G.P.), which are perhaps unusual for beginners.
Teachers will explain.

The violence of the chords makes possible the use of some distinctive tone colour, as well as for left hand
staccato. (The raising of the *barré* in producing this *staccato* also relaxes the left hand.) This is a bit unusual
in traditional technique, but is often used in jazz.